Messages From The Other Side

Stories of the Dead, Their Communication, and Unfinished Business

G.W. Mullins

ISBN: 978-1-64516-870-6

Second Edition

Light Of The Moon Publishing has allowed this work to remain exactly as the author intended, verbatim, without editorial input.

Printed in the United States of America

<u>Other titles available from G.W. Mullins include:</u>

Daniel Awakens – A Ghost Story Begins

Daniel Is Waiting A Ghost Story – From The Dead Of Night Book One

Daniel Returns - From The Dead Of Night Book Two

Star People, Sky Gods And Other Tales Of The Native American Indians

The Native American Story Book Volume 1-5- Stories Of The American Indians For Children

Walking With Spirits Volumes 1-6 Native American Myths, Legends, And Folklore

The Native American Cookbook

Cherokee A Collection of American Indian Legends, Stories And Fables

Rise Of The Snow Queen Book One - The Polar Bear King

Animal Tales Of The Native American Indians

This book is dedicated to my Great-Grandmother Myrtle who taught me that I had no reason to fear the dead.

The stories in this book are true. I have changed names and location and minor details to protect the people who have shared their stories with me.

If you are reading this book it is because you and I probably have a similar interest. We like other people want to know what happens after death. Is there something more? Do we go on? In that same line of thought, are our loved ones still with us in one way or another. I think we have a right to know and it is a healthy thing to question.

To begin with, I am not a psychic, like the late Sylvia Browne, James Van Praagh or John Edward. I don't even have a television show like Tyler Henry, to give readings to celebrities. I am an author who has seen too many things that are unexplainable. Among them, are things that hit so close to home, I need answers just like you.

So all that said, please join me on this journey through life and death. Maybe along the way something that I have learned might help you understand something you have seen or experienced. If you take anything away from this book, I'd like you to know you are not alone. There are millions of us that question if we have had a sign and if it was real. I have personally had a visitation dream and it was one of the most moving things I could ever share with you.

Let go of the fear of not being believed, because I believe you. I've been there. I have been scared to believe what I have seen was real and fear made me not tell others. I overcame that, and so can you. Thanks for coming on this journey with me.

G.W.

Table Of Contents

Introduction

My Great-Grandmother told me it was OK to believe in spirits and the dead because they are real but can't hurt you. As a child I was scared of cemeteries and the idea of ghosts. She was not; she believed that the dead are all around us, they were just "beyond the veil" as she called it. She helped me to overcome my fear. I came to realize as I got older that many did not believe the dead were still with us. Only those with an open mind are receptive to the spirits that are still with us and the messages that they may have.

There are those people who, no matter how hard they try, cannot accept what they cannot see. If it is not something provable or presentable immediately, they will not acknowledge its existence. It is those people who discredit the existence of spirits. They have not seen one, so it does not exist.

This book is an exploration of the unseen. To accept the information inside, you have to have an open mind. I don't ask you to take any of this at face value: just read and consider if you believe.

ADC = After Death Communication: Looking for Signs after the Loss of a Loved One

The sudden or unexpected loss of a loved one often leaves survivors searching for answers and resolution. In some cases of loss, such as suicide, loved ones are left devastated and have a need to know why things happened as they did. Family members need closure and knowledge that the deceased is at peace.

Regardless of religious belief, it is natural after death to want to communicate once more with the one who has passed. In most cases it is a simple need for reassurance. A person needs to know the loved one is safe while at the same time the spirit might want the loved one to know they will be OK. The reasons may differ but the need for positive closure is just human nature.

The stories of After Death Communication come from all corners of the earth. The methods may be different but the end results are often similar over cultures and different peoples. Some people see signs; some take notice of things many might say are a coincidence. Some believe you can instigate a visit by burning a candle, using personal items or even induced dreams. There are even several TV shows where mediums claim to contact lost spirits.

When my mother passed, there were signs everywhere. You could feel her presence but in so many instances, things around the house were happening in unexplainable ways. It was just too much to be a coincidence. With everything that was going on I kept feeling like I was being reassured. When I would start to worry or feel sad, something strange would happen to distract me, like lights turning off by themselves, or when I swore I heard my name called when no one was there.

The signs became pretty much a part of everyday life for a very long time for me and my stepfather. The one thing that bothered me the most was the 3 A.M. wake up calls.

My mother had a stroke which left her paralyzed on her right side. She was incapable of getting out of bed, dressing by herself or even going to the bathroom alone. So when my stepfather left at 2 A.M. to go to work, I was on call until the morning when we had someone stay with her so I could go to work.

It was almost like clockwork, at 3 A.M. there would be a knocking to get my attention to come and take her to the bathroom. It was a hard thing seeing such a mobile person unable to care for herself. I know she did not want life to be like that but sometimes in life you do what you have to. And every night I got up and took care of her and then she would go back to bed and stay until breakfast. After she died the 3 A.M. knocking continued.

The first couple of days I just brushed it off that I was dreaming it. After all, it had been my routine for months before she died. Then after about a week, I started to question the fact I still heard it. I was very grief struck by her passing, and I had a very hard time dealing with the whole situation. So my first thought was 'What is wrong with me?' I was very relieved because soon after my father had time off of work and sure enough he heard the knocking too. I felt bad for him, being I heard the knocking from down the hall, he heard it right next to him in his bedroom. I could imagine if you were not expecting it, that sound would terrify a person.

In time the odd occurrences calmed down. I did wonder why my mother did not visit me in person. I had heard of so many people who had visits and some were people close to me. But it didn't happen for months. And when the house settled down and life got back to whatever we called normal, I still waited. But you know what they say, if you stop looking for something, that is when you find it. Almost six months after my mother died, I was awakened one night to find her there. I have believed ever since that after-death communication is possible.

Is Death Really What We Understand It To Be?

Sometimes in life you have to question if what we have always been told to be true actually is reality. According to polls taken of the general public 65% of those polled believe there is some form of afterlife. Of the remaining people in the poll around 30% are sitting on the fence while 5% are skeptics. The majority of people believe - yet After Death Communication seems to be a subject we keep to ourselves.

Similar polls have been taken in the past showing that 5% of the United States has had a near death experience where the majority of them feel they experienced something they believed to be an afterlife. There have been plenty of people throughout time who have come forward with stories of their experiences with the afterlife. How could so many people have experienced something so similar and it not be true?

If we establish that there is some sort of afterlife, and death is not the final step in life, then how is it so hard to believe that communications from another level is possible. If you polled how many people believed in after death communication, it is 40 percent of the population and the number is higher (70 to 80%) if you are a spouse.

So what does all this data mean? Put simply - millions of Americans believe in the afterlife and communication with loved ones who have passed over. The afterlife is real and imminent.

When Are Spirits More Likely To Appear?

The most realistic and believable time is when you are alone.

When would be the most realistic time to get your attention than when you have no distractions and there are no other people to interfere. When you are alone you are more likely to notice a subtle shift and the presence of another.   Mornings and evenings are more ideal times for communication since you probably have fewer things going on.

As with anything to receive a message you have to be open to it and clear of mind. A clouded head will only block your ability to know what is going on. In the evenings are the most realistic times of the day, since we are winding down and releasing stress and there is less mental chatter going on.

The fewer distractions, the calmer your mind is, the better chance a loved one can get through.

When You're Sleeping/Dreaming

When you are sleeping, most times you are alone or with someone who is not distracting you. When you are in a dream, you are in an altered state of consciousness. Even if you share a bed with someone, when you awaken from sleep, you will be the only one aware of a visitation.

It is believable that a loved one would try to contact you as you sleep since this the time your brain is quiet and receptive.

During a Difficult Time In Your Life

During a time of transition and crisis is an ideal time for a visit. Your family and friends supported you in life, why is it so hard to believe they would not want to be there in the afterlife.

If you knew someone who was your rock, your means of support, or a shoulder to cry on, it is very believable they would still want to maintain this relationship with you. If you shared your life with a partner or soul mate they are not likely to stop loving you from the Other Side. These people still extend their love around us. They want to provide us comfort.

During Family Events

From weddings, to births, graduations and changes in life, your loved ones would have been there in life, and in death they would still want to be.

Sensing A Visit From A Loved One:

The 5 Most Common Ways to Feel a Spirit

Having the ability to sense a spirit is not a special gift. So many of us can do it; it just takes the ability to concentrate. If you are reading this book you probably have the desire to receive a communication and the ability to do so.

Clairsentient means having the ability to sense spirits. You may have already experienced some types of this sense before. Have you ever walked into a room and felt like you were not alone? Did you look around and think no one was there but you still felt like eyes were on you. Chances are you weren't alone. Perhaps you had someone looking in on you, or stopping by to say hi. Just because you did not see or hear them did not mean they were not there.

Sometimes the sensations are a bit more in your face. Suppose you visited a cemetery and the feeling in the air around you was heavy. Ok, it might be humidity, or maybe it is not. One of my favorites is when you go to a perfectly normal warm location and then you feel cold air surrounding you chilling you to the bone.

Some signs that you should always be aware of when spirits visit are: a quick change in temperature, an electrical charge in the air, high pressure. Take a moment and see how many of these signs you can identify with or have experienced. Then start paying attention to your surroundings and look for the signs that might be right in front of you.

Once you experience something you feel is valid, just remember this is common and being able to identify this occurrence is normal.

The Most Common Signs Of Contact From Deceased Loved Ones

There are many ways our loved ones try to connect with us. After their passing, loved ones might come to you in dreams, feelings or sensation, a familiar scent or the feeling of being touched.

There are so many reasons a loved one might return, but you don't have to be a medium or psychic to receive their messages. You only need an open mind and the ability to believe it can happen. Someone who has a closed mind and is not open to the experience is not likely to see what might be right in front of their face.

Communication can occur at any place or time, although they are most common when you are by yourself and undistracted. Being in familiar surroundings or a place where you are at ease will make contact easier. You can receive a sign or message when you are awake, in dream state, or even lucid dreaming.

The following is a list of the most common methods deceased loved ones may use to visit you.

1. Dream Visitations

A dream visitation is much different from a regular dream. In the dream state you are removed from your everyday surroundings. There aren't distractions from people, television, background noise, or everyday life. You are more receptive and on a different mental level.

In these visitation dreams, the loved one will enter the dream much like a memory. They can and will communicate with you. They are often there to reassure and comfort you. Sometimes they will ask you to deliver messages to other people. Many times they just want to let you know they are ok and put your mind at ease.

My Own Visitation From My Mother

I was 25 when my mother died. It was one of the most traumatizing experiences I have ever survived. She was one of the strongest people I had ever known. She was hardly ever ill. She was the type who took care of everyone else when they needed it. Then one day when she was 49 years old, she went to bed as normally as she ever did, but the person who awoke in the middle of the night was a different person.

She stood up to get out of bed in the middle of the night and crashed to the floor. She was in no way coherent. My stepfather tried to help her but she could not even respond to him. He called me from down the hall to tell me something was wrong and we called the ambulance immediately.

When the paramedics arrived they were sure she had suffered a stroke in her sleep. My heart sank being I had seen the result of strokes with people before. They took her to the hospital and after a time administered a drug which restored some of her functions, but not all. She was paralyzed on her right side. It affected her arm, leg and eye. I don't know if in her mind, she understood or not. We knew she would never be the same again.

There was a glimmer of the personality she once had when she was moved to a hospital room and visited by the first doctor. The man came in and greeted her and she remembered him as her doctor, when she had been pregnant a couple of years before. He asked her the questions they had to, to establish if she was coherent. She passed the date, and then do you know your name. But when he got to president of the United States, she had decided she was through with the question game. He asked and she told him it was J. Edger Hoover. She looked up at him with a sarcastic look on her face as he realized she was trying to smile at him. We all knew at that point she was still fighting.

In time, the doctors did all they could do, but rehabilitation could only correct so much and she had to face life confined to a wheel chair. When she came home, she was for the most part, mentally capable. We learned in time she was different, and the loving caring woman who went to bed that night had been changed to a person who was scared and at times would be like someone we had never known.

It was hard to watch the woman who had been so active before becoming this new person. She was an artist who made so many beautifully painted pieces and so many wonderful sculptures. She was always on the go and loved life. She would have done anything to help someone who needed it. In one night all that was gone.

Months came and went; and so did so many therapy sessions. Along the way there seemed to be some progress but it did not come quickly. She tried so hard to walk but even with a brace it was too dangerous. She could no longer paint or sculpt being her right hand was for the most part unusable.

Six months came and went and I would like to say they were easy, but they were a learning experience. One I wish I had never had to go through. When a parent is totally dependent, life changes for everyone. We worked in shifts to care for her and when we had to work, friends came to stay and help her out. She seemed to enjoy having friends around.

The holidays were her favorite time of the year and we made an effort to make sure she had the best year ever. When February came, I was baking a cake for my stepfather's birthday and she was trying to help. About half way through, she said to me, "I won't be needing a cake this year." I asked her what she meant but she would not say anything.

The beginning of March arrived and things changed. On the first Sunday of the month she was sitting with her breakfast and not trying to eat. That should have been the first warning sign. And then she had the second stroke. She fell over sideways as we rushed to her side. In the hospital, the doctor said she had definitely had a second stroke and she had to stay at the hospital.

She came out of it for a while and pleaded with us to take her home. The doctor said there was no way he could allow it. So we left her there. Trust me, I never felt so bad before.

My stepfather stayed with her in the hospital for the next couple of days. The week before her birthday she had a third stroke, this time on the other side of her brain. The doctors did all the tests and determined she was brain dead. All the medicine in the world could not fix this. The family came in and as in times of crisis, the in-fighting began.

The doctors wanted to remove my mother from life support. The family split in two and war broke out in the hospital. They went to my stepfather who agreed to remove her from life support, and then they came to me.

The doctor took me away, sat down with me and told me that I had to make the decision. For some reason it had all been left up to me. I chose to remove life support since my mother had a Living Will that stated she did not want to be kept alive that way. In one afternoon I lost the majority of my family, but I respected my mother's last wishes.

I had a hard time dealing with everything. I was inconsolable at the funeral. On a good day I could drive to work without crying and having to pull the car over to the side of the road. I remembered how Great-Grandma told me about spirits coming back to say good-bye or pass on messages. I spoke with her about this and how I had not gotten a message from my mother. She just told me to give it time, it would happen. I felt bad for Great-

Grandma, she was now over 100 years old and she had been there when her daughter died and now her grand-daughter.

Months passed and I healed but the pain never really went away. I had to go on with life and it was very different now. I had adopted a son and my stepfather was living with me. My focus was on so many new things. One night I went to bed and finally dozed off when I felt a gentle nudge like someone was trying to get my attention. I sat up to see my mother standing before me.

I did not see the person before me as a ghost, she was just my mom. I was so happy but so confused. I asked her why she had not come to see me sooner and she said I had to deal with my pain first or I might not have seen her. We talked and for a short time it was like she was still with me. She looked just as she did before the stroke, a happy, healthy woman full of life. She said at the end she had to go but she had a message for my stepfather. As she left I remember this feeling of peace and happiness washing over me. I sat up in my bed and could smell her perfume all around me. It was like a comforting hug.

For a long time I did not tell anyone what had happened. I think the change in my personality might have given me away. Her visit gave me the strength to let go of a lot of the pain. I still miss her and the hurt will never be gone completely but it is different now. In time I opened up about what had happened and I tried to pass the message that was left for my stepfather but for some reason I blocked it out. Then one day, my stepfather after decades of being an alcoholic, decided to give it, and smoking up. I just remembered the message like someone put it back into my head. She had told me to tell him she was sorry for everything that had happened.

I never got another visit from my mother but I feel as if she is around and watching over my family. Little things have happened from time to time that have told me she was there.

Shortly after she died we could not find her insurance policy. We looked everywhere and as we were giving up, we decided to go to dinner. When we came back my father headed for the bar which was his daily routine. When he sat down, there, where his glass was about to be put down, was the insurance policy waiting for him. We didn't question it or the many unusual things that happened since. It was just nice to know she was still around.

A Father's Message to His Son

Just a quick message before you read this section. I totally believe in organized religion and that people should be allowed to believe in whatever they wish to. In this section, the people I write about were attending a church that was very controlling and cult like. Their lives were controlled on a very unhealthy level. It is not my intention to make anyone who believes in religion feel bad or take offense. After having first-hand experience with this group, I did fear for the safety of some of the people who participated in this church. Please keep that in mind when you read and realize I am not saying religion is bad, perhaps just some people are.

I have a friend I am very close to. We have known each other for over a decade and we share everything. I had told him of my belief in the dead and messages but he never talked much about his own experiences until a few weeks after his father died.

Larry was always very close to his parents. Growing up he was raised very religious and taught never to question the ways of the little country church he attended. The trouble was, as he got older, he realized the control the small church had over his parents was almost to the level of a cult. The preacher decided what was right for everyone, such as women were not allowed to cut their hair, or wear jewelry (including wedding rings). Many of the women made their own clothes since fashionable things were supposedly adornment and the devil's work. The preacher did not believe in television and he didn't expect anyone to have a TV in their home. Larry's family did not buy a TV until 2001 after the attacks of 9/11 and it was then out of fear of terrorism. As he began to question this life, he realized he had to get away from it. He was sure his only escape was college.

As Larry graduated high school, which was actually the church school since he was not allowed to interact with many of the local people, he announced that he was planning to go to college. His parents quickly shot this down, and told him if he planned on going to school he would never get any money from them and he would be on his own. Many of the church goers were uneducated and the preacher liked it that way, but Larry was not going to take "no" for an answer. He got a job and earned as much money as he could and started college.

As time went on, Larry was very successful with his college and went on to a major university. He got married and had a family of his own. His father tried to change his way of thinking, if for no other reason to still have is son in his life. Larry's mother however rebelled at every step trying to cause problems for him. She only had time for her church and her misguided belief.

Larry's relationship with his father strengthened over time and realizing she had lost the battle for control, the mother tried to find a peaceful level they could all exist in.

After years of battling, Larry visited home again and over the next decade found that there was a change in his old home. His leaving made his parents change and they began to understand the life they had led was not always the best one. Although the mother still attended the church, the father did not. The church itself was forced to change as well as the younger children grew up, they followed by example and got out and went to school and many did not come back to the church.

Larry's parents were much older than what you would expect. His father was over fifty when he was born and his mother was in her late forties. So growing up, many people thought they were his grandparents. By the time he was in his late twenties his parents were elderly. His father's health was not very good. He had worked all of his life, first as a farmer and then later as a truck driver. The years had taken their toll on him. When he was in his late seventies, he had a stroke. He was never cooperative about going to hospitals. It might have been from the prior church beliefs. The preacher told them that hospitals were not in god's plan. If you were meant to die, then it was your time.

When Larry was about to be born, the church had a midwife to help his mother give birth. As she attempted to deliver, the midwife figured out he was breach and could not be delivered. At first, they were not going to call the hospital, but they went against church belief and asked for help. It was the beginning of many of the church goers insisting on hospitalization for pregnancy. This did not please the preacher, his word had been challenged and he let them all know about it in Sunday sermons.

After a large fight and a refused ambulance call, Larry's mother insisted they go to the hospital and it was there they diagnosed that the father had suffered a stroke. They treated him and started medications to heal him. He was not paralyzed and at first he seemed pretty normal, but as time passed they noticed that mentally he would slip from time to time.

When the father came home, he tried to resume normal life but working his old job as a truck driver was not possible. He retired and although he should have been able to fall back on his retirement the company he worked for had not paid their taxes properly and his retirement was seized with all the company's assets. As the stress of being forced to live this new lifestyle got harder on the family, the father's health declined. His behavior became more erratic and he would say odd things or do things totally out of character.

Out if the blue one day he decided they needed a new car and went to the local car lot and as his wife watched, he signed for a very expensive overpriced vehicle.

Larry's mother just stood by and obeyed her husband as the church had taught her to do. It was not long after that the father developed Gallstones. His ability to go to the bathroom was affected and although they knew there was a problem for months they ignored it until an infection spread throughout his body.

The day he could not get off the couch, he was taken to the hospital, where for over the course of a week he had another stroke, and went into a coma. The doctors didn't see much hope and called in the family to pay last respects. Although he was very ill at the time with a severe case of the flu, Larry went to the hospital to see his father hooked up to machines and tubes. It was more than he could take. He was destroyed to see what had been allowed to go so badly.

Larry's mind flashed back to the days of his childhood when his father would allow him to go to work with him on the big truck. They would fly down the road together just the two of them. He missed those days now. When he left that day Larry was sure he would never see his father again.

When Larry arrived home his mother called hour after hour and day after day. She panicked and blamed herself since she did not get him the care he needed. Larry's condition got worse and he was borderline pneumonia. The stress of the situation took its toll on him and he could not deal with the stress. As the father was treated for the infection the doctor's decided to put in a breathing tube. As they did, the father went into cardiac arrest and for a moment died.

The doctors brought him back but decided it was a losing battle. It was just days before Christmas and they decided to try to keep him alive until after the holidays. The 26 of December was Larry's parent's anniversary. The mother decided that the day after they could remove the machines. In a matter of hours Russell was dead.

Larry got the phone call early in the morning. He was barely coherent due to his own illness. He was in no condition to travel. He stayed that way for over a week following. The funeral came and went and he could not attend for fear of his own health. He seemed eerily calm and did not cry much after the time his father died. His spouse was concerned he was not dealing with it at all but he insisted he would be alright.

When his health improved Larry went to visit the gravesite. For the first time as he read the writing on the stone, he cried and finally said good-bye to his father. As he walked away from the grave he played it all over in his mind and knew it could have been prevented. It was becoming no secret that he blamed his mother for much of the situation.

When Larry returned home he tried to get on with his normal life. He talked to me about the situation and realized he was glad not to see the end of his father's life in person. He was fortunate enough to have memories of his father alive, not dying or dead. He just wished he could have said good-bye in person.

A couple of weeks went passed and he came to me. He said he needed to talk about something and he was not sure if I would believe him. He told me of the night before, he went to bed and was fast asleep and then it happened.   He woke up but he was not in his bed. He was standing by a road somewhere in the country. It was a bright sunny day and the place was peaceful. As he walked towards the road a big truck pulled up and as he looked inside he saw his father driving.

Russell asked Larry if he was going to get in as if he was joking. Larry got in the passenger seat and the truck pulled off and they road together and talked. The conversation was nothing in general just every day father and son talk. As the truck pulled around back to where Larry had gotten in, he opened the door and prepared to leave. Larry leaned into the window and said "Dad, I love you." His father smiled and said he loved him too.

As Larry walked down the path beside the road he looked back at his father. He smiled as his father waved to him. Then the big truck revved up and pulled away driving into the bright sunlight. Larry turned away as soon as the truck was gone. He walked a bit and then blinked his eyes and he was at home again.

As Larry told me the story, he was scared I would think he was crazy or making it up. He said he didn't want me to think he was copying something I had experienced when my mother died. I assured him I believed him, and I did, because I had been there myself. He told me that he felt so good when it was all over. He was happy that he could say good-bye in person and tell his dad he loved him.

Larry did not see his dad again after that but he was OK with the fact he was able to have one last ride with his dad. He knew his dad was at peace and they both finished unfinished business.

2. Sensing Their Presence

Many people believe they have sensed loved ones around them after their passing.

You might have noticed a shift in the feel of what you consider normal – something like a change of energy or mood. It could be as simple as a cold feeling in certain areas that should not be cold. When you are sitting in a room you might feel as if someone is sitting beside you. If the person was someone you were close to, you probably have a sense of what is normal for them to be near you. This feeling is second nature, especially if they were a loved one or a spouse. Think of it as what you perceive to be their presence. When they were alive they could come into a room and you probably knew they were there before you looked. That feeling can still be felt as a spirit visitation. This is a common type of visit.

Your loved one has the same essence they had when alive, and now in the afterlife.

My Stepfather's Mother Stopped By - To Say Good-bye

I was young when my mother remarried. I have to admit it was a rocky road being uprooted to move to a different state and saying good-bye to friends. My mother and I lived in a mountain community when I was younger, so when she told me we were going to move to a major city to live with my stepfather, I was terrified.

We did move and life was new and different and with the new, came my stepfather's family. We had a ton of new relatives who instantly started to come around all the time. My stepfather's mother Myrtle was elderly and she and her husband moved to be close locally to my stepfather. For a while this situation worked until it was decided they really could not live on their own. So they were sent to a home where they could be cared for. I did not understand the concept, in my family, since I was a child we always took care of the elderly and they just went to live with a relative.

As the months passed Myrtle's health went downhill. We really didn't know how long she had left, so we prepared ourselves with what was to come. My stepfather was his usual 'I am not going to let this get to me' self. He tried not to show emotion that often. You could tell inside he was scared.

One night when we were all home getting settled in for the night, my stepfather was in the kitchen getting a drink while I was in my room and my mother was in her room just a few feet away from me. I heard movement and just assumed it was one of them. I went about my business getting my stuff ready for school the next morning when I felt really uneasy like I was being watched.

I looked at the windows but the curtains were closed and no one could see in. Then I went to the door. Just as I approached I saw the edge of a flowing red cloth pass by as if it was blowing in the breeze. I opened the door quickly to catch a glimpse of a woman moving down the hall and on her way to the kitchen. I assumed it was my mother.

As I headed out the door and walked towards the open hall, I looked up to see my mother coming to her doorway. I cocked my head and looked at her until she demanded to know what was wrong with me. I told her I was sure I saw her walking in the hall in a red night gown. She pulled at what she was wearing which was blue and assured me she had been wearing it since she prepared for bed.

I told her whatever or whoever it was had headed for the kitchen. We both headed there to find my stepfather finishing his drink. I asked if he had seen the woman in red and he looked at me like I was nuts and told me there was no one in the house but us and the dog. I just couldn't understand why I was the only one who saw this woman.

The next morning the call came from the home. Myrtle had died during the night. They said she had gone peacefully and happily wearing the new red night gown her son had bought her. We never spoke about the woman in red again but we all knew who it was. I was glad to know who it was, but after the incident I learned to fear what I might not be seeing.

3. Feelings of Being Touched

Simple gestures might be used to let you know a loved one is near you. It might be something as simple as a hug, a touch of your hair, touching your hand, or even a hand on your shoulder when you are alone – sometimes communication can come in the most comforting of ways.

Touch is a very common way of comforting from a spirit in the days following a passing. Your loved one is simply trying to comfort you in your time of grief. Many people who are too deep in grief cannot notice these supportive gestures simply because they are not receptive.

In some cases these visits and communication may last long after passing. This communication may not just consist of attempt to touch you but objects around you to get your attention. You might notice objects appearing in weird places or things disappearing and reappearing later.

A Touch on the Shoulder

When I moved into my new house, it was a major undertaking. The place needed tons of work, almost to the level of rebuilding and remodeling the whole interior. I had gotten the place for an amazing price, and after getting settled in, I realized I would be paying in so many other ways.

Just as my family had settled, the rains began. Little did we know the storm coming would be one of the most devastating in the area. After days of heavy rain, thunder and lightning, the flood came. Much of the area was under water and getting around would be almost impossible, so we went to work on the house. We had fortunately gotten all the work supplies in just before the rain began.

The work went slow, but since we had plenty of time… Settling in we only used a couple of rooms of the house and worked from one room to another in remodeling. The work was hard and at times I wondered why I would take on such a challenge. More than once I went off by myself and just sat on the staircase that led to the second floor. The more stressed I became, the more I noticed little things began to happen in the house.

The first days it was innocent enough, I would look for my hammer and it would not be where I left it. Then my screw driver disappeared from the table in front of me and would end up in a weird place like the kitchen stove. At first I brushed it off like I was just tired and forgetful but after a while it became a regular routine I just couldn't overlook. I asked my family and they all had no idea what I was talking about.

I began having the feeling I was being watched by someone but had no idea by who. Things went on happening until one day I had reached the end of my rope and yelled out that whoever was messing with my tools, needed to leave them alone. Over the rest of that day things seemed to turn up around the house in the weirdest of places. At the end of the day, I made my way to my favorite seat at the third step up the staircase and with a level of complete exhaustion, I put my hands up to my face and leaned forward ready to collapse.

Just as I was thinking about getting up, I felt the sensation on my back. It started out softly, then I was sure there was a hand resting on my shoulder. At first, I just felt it was one of the family trying to comfort me. Then I realized no one was upstairs and I would have heard them coming down. I slowly pulled my hands down and with a level of fear turned my head to see who was behind me. To my surprise there was nothing there.

I was scared to say anything about it to my spouse. I was sure I would be laughed at. It was too weird a thing to have happen. When I did make mention of it, I realized the feeling was familiar. My mother used to put her hand on my shoulder like that all the time when she was alive. I am not sure it was her, but I hope it was. I'm not really sure I like the idea of it being touched by someone else.

4. Smelling a Familiar Scent

Clairgustance is the ability to smell a scent of a deceased person.

Scents are all around us and sometimes we associate a certain smell with a person. Whether it is a smell of perfume, or just the way a person's hair smells you associate it with that person. Sometimes you might remember a person as a smoker or the smell of smoke, you might think of your uncle as a cigar smoker that smoked sweet smelling cigars. If you smelled that cigar in a place where no one smokes and you are alone, maybe your uncle has come for a visit.

Grandma's Perfume

I heard about a woman who was very close to her grandmother. When the grandmother died, the woman was devastated. She got very depressed and closed herself off from everyone for weeks. Nothing could console her. Then one day, as she lay in bed, she smelled something familiar. It was the smell of lavender. It was the same as the perfume her grandmother wore all the time.

The subtle smell broke her depression. Although she did not see her grandmother, the smell made her realize there was a presence.

5. Hearing the Voice of a Loved One

Clairaudience is the experience of hearing a spirit's voice. It is possible to hear voices of the deceased. Sometimes it is like the person is still in the room with you and at other times it is internally. Internal clairaudience is the most common form or communication.   Many times people talk out loud to loved ones who have passed. If the spirit is present, is it so absurd to believe they would not answer?

The next time you speak to a loved one, keep an open mind and listen.

My Stepfather's Escape

My stepfather left the city shortly after my mother's death. He was not happy there without her, so he headed for the country. He was into being alone and fishing, so he found a house where he could do both. There was only one other house near his and the isolation was therapeutic for him.

He had been settled in for a couple of months before I came to the area to see him. He seemed to be happy to see me and I was relieved he had adjusted so well. The country setting was calm and quiet with hardly any noise. I began to realize how the lack of city sounds was so different.

One day, my stepfather and I went shopping. We were gone for hours before returning. As we pulled into the driveway, he stopped to get the mail as I headed into the house. As I opened the kitchen door I heard the voices. At first, I worried we had left the TV on, but the sound was not right. I stopped in fear thinking someone had broken into the house.

As I moved slowly in the dining room and got ready to turn to the right and head to the living room the voices stopped. I spun around and looked all around and looked into one room after another but there was no one. The house was empty.

My stepfather entered the house and I told him what had happened. He smiled at me and shook his head and said "So you have heard them too." He had heard them on so many occasions and the voices always ended as soon as he got to the dining room. The voices were never intelligible, just a little louder than a whisper and always out of sync.

Over the time I was there I heard the voices several times but could never figure out what was being said. They came at a different time of the day and night. We never figured out who they were but it sounded like more than one person and a mix of male and female.

6. Unexpected Electrical Activity

We are surrounded by energy. People are a form of energy and the appliances and items we use every day are electrical.

It is not a big leap to believe that a spirit who is a form of energy can use devices that are run by electricity. Whether to use to send a message, just to get your attention, or just to relieve frustration of not being heard it is believable spirits can cause electrical disturbances.

The most common devices reported throughout history that can be disturbed by a spirit are TV's, lights, and toys. Whether it is changing channels, turning lights on and off, or making toys move, these are all effective forms of communication.

7. Phone Calls from the Other Side

My stepfather died a very unexpected and unusual death at home. No one expected it or was ready to deal with his passing. After he was taken away and all the insanity slowed a bit, my cell phone rang. The sound of the ring tone chilled me to the bone. Every family member had their own song programmed; the one playing was my stepfather's. When I worked up the nerve to answer, there was nothing. I said hello but there was no response and then my phone returned itself to the main screen as if the call was ended at the other end.

I looked this up online and learned there were people from all around the world who had similar experiences. In the days following the death of loved ones their phones often went off with either no one on the line or a static sound. The phone is an electrical device so it is not hard to believe a spirit could manipulate it. In the age of cell phones, simple manipulation of the power in the phone can easily dial a number.

8. Receiving a Symbolic, Message, or Sign

Spirits are probably eager to let you know they are with you and still a part of your life. Their messages will come when you least expect it.

While sometimes their messages are hard to perceive, some people can feel their loved ones around them, watching over them. Spirits will provide us with signs, some less obvious, while others we cannot ignore.

A Gift from the Dearly Departed

When my mother died, our house was in total chaos. She was the one who handled the bills, important papers and made all the decisions while my stepfather worked. So when she died we had no idea where important papers were especially her life insurance papers.

We tore the house apart looking for the papers since we needed them to file a claim and pay for her funeral. After achieving total exhaustion we decided to go out for dinner. I was at the end of my rope and so was my stepfather.

When we came home it was late and neither of us had the energy to search any longer so we decided to call it. My stepfather walked into the kitchen and sat down on the bar stool that was behind the counter that separated the kitchen from the living room, which he did all the time. As he looked down at the counter that had been totally clear when we left, there were the papers we had been looking for the whole time. We both agreed my mother had to have been watching us and gave us a helping hand.

So long story short, spirits will send us messages and help that we cannot ignore. People will try to tell you it is coincidence and not a message from the other side. These people have either not experienced something like this or are just closed minded. Don't let anyone tell you not to believe!

The signs can and will come to you in a variety of ways, and the key is keep your eye open for anything out of the ordinary.

So what and where should you look for signs?

Spirits like to clue us in with things that were important to them in life. My mother loved music boxes. She had several and my aunt Mary had a huge display case full of them. Whenever my mother would visit her, she always headed for the cabinet and would wind the music boxes. It was a habit she had and she did it every time she visited Mary.

After my mother's death, Mary was devastated and often stayed home not wanting to interact with others. Weeks after the funeral Mary called me and told me the music boxes had started playing on their own.

At first I wondered if maybe it was temperature change making the internal works release and start playing. After the second and third night I began to get the hint. My uncle didn't believe the boxes were playing at all until they started to play while he was there as well. The music boxes continued to play for weeks until Mary made it through her grief and started to get out again.

Maybe it was coincidence or just my mother's way of nudging Mary to let go of her grief.

9. Movement

Sometimes spirits will cause things to move to get your attention. Sometimes a photo will continue to fall over or drop from the wall. Do you keep losing your keys even though you know where you put them down? This could be a way of communication that even a person who is in denial cannot ignore. Moving objects also cause noise and that may not be so easily ignored.

Joey's New Playmate

When I moved into my new house all sorts of weird things happened while we got settled and worked on the place. These weird things went on for the better part of the first two years. One of the weirdest things was Joey's new playmate.

Joey is our Newfoundland dog. He is like a big ball of fur, and I do mean big being he is over 135lbs. As we moved into the house we stayed mostly on the lower floor since the house was being completely remodeled. Joey however did not get the memo about not going up to the second floor. And as we worked, he would escape the noise and debris by running for the stairs. He hated loud noises and the saw was not his friend.

Joey was not one to run and play by himself, he preferred one of us to play rope with him or bounce a ball. If he was not playing, he mainly liked to curl up and be near us. As the days went on, we noticed more and more he was upstairs. Then the weird noises came.

We would hear him running back and forth like he was playing with someone. At first we were happy he was having fun in his new house, then we became aware he was doing things he would never do. As he began bouncing like he was rough housing with someone holding his rope. We decided to look into it. You just don't overlook something as heavy as Joey bouncing on the floor above you.

As we watched him he was distracted as if he could see something we could not. When we ruled out other animals and that we were truly the only ones in the house, we decided he should stay downstairs. We blocked the stairs and made sure he could not go anywhere we could not see.

Everything was relatively calm until one night when we were watching TV. As I sat beside Joey I watched him and saw he kept looking at the stairs. Then he did something that scared me. As I watched his eyes and head, he moved his head up the stairs like he was watching someone climb one stair at a time. The fear I had as a child came back and stayed a while.

One day a man came around and said he had been the gardener when the previous owner lived there. I learned too much that day about my new house. The woman who had lived there also died there on the second floor. But what really scared me, was she always had a large group of animals she cared for. She especially loved playing with the dogs.

Shortly after this I politely told her I owned the house and if she didn't mind we would like privacy in our new home. After that, Joey seemed pretty calm with his new home. One thing that bothered me was they sold me a house and no one said there had been a dead body found there,

10. Seeing a Spirit or Something You Cannot Explain

Seeing a spirit or apparition when you are awake with your eyes open is the least common method. It is hard to believe but it is true. So many movies show people interacting with ghosts, and even though there is a vast history of this happening, it is not common.

Just because your loved one is not appearing to you in full form does not mean they are not with you. They have probably tried another method of communication.

Many people believe that visits from their loved ones are common in the days, weeks and months following their deaths. Some people believe these visits can go on for years. This is normal. If you have a life partner or soul mate, even a child that died young, they are attached to you and will still want to be in your life.

Why Don't Some Spirits Communicate with Us?

Sometimes the issue with communication is just at our end. We are not prepared or ready to accept a message from our loved ones. It is not that we do not want to. It could be that we are just not emotionally ready. There are a variety of reasons why some spirits don't or can't communicate with us.

Death is an adjustment period for the living. Look at it from another point of view; it is a much bigger adjustment for our departed loved one. In some cases spirits might not even know they have died. They probably need help in understanding. Just as we are confused on what has just happened, they are probably confused as to what will happen from that point on.

It is not unbelievable that a spirit will need time to adjust. If the loved one was ill and died in a coma or in their sleep, it might be a shock to them. If they regained some form of consciousness, would they know they had died? What if a person died who had mental issues, would they necessarily understand how to communicate in an effective way? There are so many factors that might change what is possible in communication.

Probably the best excuse for not communicating it the realization that at the time it is not in your best interest. Grief, even though it is a hard thing, is a valuable life lesson.

Another factor to take into consideration is that we are bound by the constraints of time. We are human and bound to bodies and the earth which has a system of time. If you are a spirit, you are no longer bound to this system. Perhaps in their existence time passes at another speed and what might seem like months to us may very well feel like days to them.

Although the many things I have mentioned are rare, most spirits probably do have a desire to communicate with the living. In most cases they probably want us to know they are Ok and safe. So, even though they want to communicate with us, things at our end may get in the way and prevent the message from getting across.

Reasons Why Some Spirit Communications Aren't Received

Dreams are something most of us have all the time. Sometimes we remember them and other times they pass within the minutes we are waking up. We might experience something wonderful such as a dream or symbol but we just ignore it and write it off.

When dealing with death and being deeply bereaved comes a wall of sadness, emotion and sometimes depression. These are strong emotions to deal with. Even the strongest of us lose these battles. Just as we are often not able to deal with other people during this time, we might not allow a message from a spirit to get to us either. We just erect a wall that is impenetrable. In time when our grief releases a bit them it is more likely a message can get through.

As with anything, communication can be frustrating. We all want immediate answers, but what if it does not come for weeks, months or years. What can be more frustrating is finding out another loved one or friend got a message you had so hoped for. You have to wonder "why them" and not me. Depending on your state of mind, you may not be receptive and the other person may be. The spirit might not be contacting this person for any other reason than to just get a message across because they cannot get to you first. They are simply doing what they can to say they are alright.

Just a reminder, don't make demands or expect miracles of the spirit. Spirits are probably capable of many wonderful things but expecting them to perform on command, probably does not work into the grand scheme of things. Just because you want a certain thing to happen does not mean they are actually capable. We had to learn how to do everything in life like drive a car, or ride a bike. Wouldn't it make sense they would have to learn how to manipulate energy or learn how to communicate? In the end it is probably the spirits choice in communication, and should be on their terms. Just have faith that if they can communicate, they probably will.

A reminder, negative emotions will be the biggest hurdle to overcome in communication. If you have an issue or are hurt that someone left, then you need to deal with the anger or pain. When your mind is at ease and these feelings are gone, you will be most open to a message. So, resolve your anger, it is good for you and the spirit. A little forgiveness goes a long way for everyone involved.

The Healing Power of a Visitation Dream

There is probably nothing more healing than a visitation dream. As a person who has experienced one, I can testify to how incredibly comforting it is to see a loved one again this way. When you take the concept of this comfort and pair with the ability to see this person one on one again, it is one of the most treasured moments you will ever have. Seeing my mother one last time pulled me out of my depression and showed me she was still with me just in a new way. I know she watches over me, just like she always did.

Dreams of our loved ones also offer us a glimpse into life after death. If there is communication, they there is proof death is not the end of the road.

After-death communication has so many benefits, but the greatest would have to be that we are reassured that we really never die. We just move on to a new way of life. When our time comes we simply change the scenery and go.

I wish that everyone could have the wonderful experience I have had. Just remember every time we go to sleep at night we have the capacity to dream. We may not always remember them but they are there. Who knows, maybe when you go to bed tonight you will remember that one dream that will change your life and make you believe.

Messages through Dreams

Based On True Stories

A Grandmothers Farewell

When I was really young about 6 or 7 years old my Grandmother got really sick. We knew it was serious but no one thought she might die from the illness. I went to sleep one night and my grandmother came into my room and talked to me. She wanted me to follow her, so I did. As we walked she kept looking back over her shoulder to see if I was there. We went out of our home and into the back yard where I saw her with other people including family members. As I walked up to them, she waved goodbye to me and smiled. I told her good-bye and I loved her.

I didn't understand what had happened. I just remember waking up the next morning in my bed as always. I was off early to school and everything seemed normal. When my dad came to pick me up later that afternoon he told me grandma had died the night before.

As I got older I heard stories of how some people know they are going to die before they really do. Some of them send messages. I'm not sure if grandma had passed before she visited me or what. I am glad I could say good-bye.

Grandpa's Visit

When I was about 8 years old my Grandfather died. He was much older and it was not an unexpected thing. It hit me hard since he was like a best friend to me. My parents worked a lot and I would stay with him during times no one was home. Needless to say he was a big part of my life.

I remember his funeral and how so many people came to his and Grandma's house to pay their respects. Even though the house was overcrowded, no one sat in Grandpa's chair. We all knew it was his favorite place to watch TV or read his paper. So we respected the fact it was his.

As the time got later and it was almost evening, a lot of people left and the few that remained hung out together in the dining room where the food was. I couldn't handle the crowd so I headed for the front porch. I needed air.

As I walked past Grandpa's chair, out of the corner of my eye I saw him there. It was like he always was, reading his paper. Without thinking I said hi to him and headed for the door. As my hand touched the knob I realized what had happened.

I felt sick for a second then I turned around to see if anyone was there. The chair was empty except for a newspaper.

Russell's Grandmother

In the days back when people had wells in the back of houses for the water my Grandmother died an awful death. She was alone in the house and she was very frail. She knew she wasn't supposed to move around a lot but she was stubborn and headstrong. She went to get water one day and fell in the well. When the family got home they looked for her and they found her there.

Everyone was really upset and they did not speak of the incident much for it was too traumatizing. But after that we kept hearing noises. Most of the time it came late at night, and always on the lower level of the house.

One night I got up to go to the bathroom and I heard it. So went down and the sound was coming from the area of the well. As I approached I felt like I was being watched. The noise kept going until I was sure where it was coming from.

So every night after that the same noises happened. Something had to be done. We all talked about it and in the end we decided that maybe she was trying to say we needed to put a lid on the well so no one else would get hurt.

The following day we capped it off. It was a good idea since there were kids running round and we didn't want them to get hurt as well. That night the sounds stopped. Maybe it was just Grandma's way of sending us the message.

Alarm Clock from the Other Side

My mother would always wake me up for everything. I was a hard sleeper and she knew I would sleep through the alarm. She did it through school, and into college. When I went away after school in the military, she would tell me she missed waking me up, but I reminded her I had others who did it there.

When I settled down after the military I got married and started a family of my own. Life was pretty good and I got a good job. Trouble was I got a job that started at 2 A.M. and it was too much for me. My wife hated the early time I had to get up and leave and she was just as hard to get up as I was. And then it happened I overslept one time and it was a mad dash to get to work on time.

We talked about it when I got home and I told my wife I needed some way of getting up. This was too good a job to loose just because of being late. That night when we went to sleep, I sat the alarm and put it right by my head so I had to hear it.

Just before 2 A.M. came, something weird happened. There was a bang at the front door. When I heard it, I jumped up in the bed and so did my wife. We were startled and worried at who would be banging on our door. She looked out the window which was at the head of our bed. From it we could see the front porch, but no one was there.

The next night the same thing happened again. This went on for years and every time we looked there was nothing. After a while I got used to being awakened at this time and I could wake up to the sound of the clock. I was never late again. I have to wonder if it was my mother doing what she always did. I don't know if it was her or not but I did appreciate the help.

Grandpa's Visit

I had a visit from my grandfather shortly after he died. It seemed so real like I was really seeing him. It only lasted a few minutes but it shocked me so much I woke up.

In the dream I was visiting my Grandfather. It was not that odd, I did it all the time. I was dressed very formally in a suit and tie. I hardly ever wore things like this but my Grandfather liked it when I did. When I entered the living room my Grandfather was sitting on the couch looking very neatly dressed like he always did in his dress shirt and pants.

Everything was pretty normal until he spoke to me. His speech was normal and

I found that odd since he had a stroke years ago and his speech was always impaired.

In the dream I remember he complimented me on how good I looked and said I must have learned something from him. He hugged me and told me he loved me. As I pulled away I looked at him and told him I had worn the suit to his funeral. He told me he knew. I woke up instantly not knowing what to think. Maybe it was his way of saying he approved.

The Fire in the Bathroom

We always felt like we were not alone in our house. Maybe someone watched over us or it was a past resident. The neighbor boy I was friends with told me an older woman who had lived in the house before us had died there. After a little research I discovered she had died in my room and that creeped me out a little.

From time to time I would swear I would see something out of the corner of my eye moving about the place but I just couldn't prove it. I told my Mom and she thought I was nuts. She just laughed it off. I still chose to believe what I was seeing.

Late one night I was awakened by a weird noise coming from the hall. I was already paranoid about the house, so weird noises did not help at all. But I still went to see what was going on. As I walked towards the bathroom I smelled smoke. My father was a smoker and was forever leaving lit cigarettes in the ashtrays.

As I opened the door to the bathroom it was filled with smoke. I went in and saw the source of the smoke was from a fire in the ashtray. As I tried to dump the whole thing into the toilet, I felt a weird feeling like someone was at the door behind me. As I prepared to flush I turned and saw the older woman in the doorway for a split second.

I didn't know her. She was not a family member. I don't know why she was looking out for us but she made sure I got the fire before it got worse. At that point I wasn't scared of the house anymore. We had a protector and didn't even know it.

Coming Soon: Crossing Over

A second part to *Messages From The Other Side*